HISTORY'S GREATEST DISASTERS

HURRICANE KATRINA

by Peggy Caravantes

Published by ABDO Publishing Company, PO Box 398166, Minneapolis, MN 55439. Copyright © 2014 by Abdo Consulting Group, Inc. International copyrights reserved in all countries. No part of this book may be reproduced in any form without written permission from the publisher. The Core Library™ is a trademark and logo of ABDO Publishing Company.

Printed in the United States of America,
North Mankato, Minnesota
042013
092013
♻ THIS BOOK CONTAINS AT LEAST 10% RECYCLED MATERIALS.

Editor: Blythe Hurley
Series Designer: Becky Daum

Library of Congress Control Number: 2013931969

Cataloging-in-Publication Data
Caravantes, Peggy.
 Hurricane Katrina / Peggy Caravantes.
   p. cm. -- (History's greatest disasters)
ISBN 978-1-61783-958-0 (lib. bdg.)
ISBN 978-1-62403-023-9 (pbk.)
Includes bibliographical references and index.
1. Hurricane Katrina, 2005--Juvenile literature. 2. Hurricanes--United States--Juvenile literature.   I. Title.
363.34--dc23
                                        2013931969

Photo Credits: Bill Haber/AP Images, cover, 1, 36; NOAA/AP Images, 4; Lynne Sladk/AP Images, 6; J. Pat Carter/AP Images, 8; Mari Darr-Welch/AP Images, 10; Chuck Burton/AP Images, 12; Eric Gay/AP Images, 14; Edward A. Ornelas/San Antonio Express-News/AP Images, 16; Red Line Editorial, Inc., 17, 19; Dave Martin/AP Images, 20; Vincent Laforet/AP Images, 22, 45; John Davenport/San Antonio Express-News/AP Images, 25; Pat Sullivan/AP Images, 26; Robert F. Bukaty/AP Images, 28, 34; David J. Phillip/AP Images, 30; USGS/AP Images, 32; Alex Brandon/AP Images, 39; Rob Carr/AP Images, 40

CONTENTS

CHAPTER ONE

A STORM IS BORN

It had no name when it was born in the Caribbean. The date was August 23, 2005. Beginning as a group of dark clouds and rain, the storm had winds of less than 39 miles per hour (63 km/h). Scientists who study the weather, called meteorologists, said it was a tropical depression. As it developed stronger winds on August 24, the tropical depression was declared a tropical storm and given the name Katrina.

This image of the enormously destructive storm that was to become Hurricane Katrina was taken from outer space.

While most people dread the coming of tropical storms and hurricanes, this Florida surfer is waiting to hit the waves while storm clouds gather on the horizon.

Tropical storm Katrina battered the Bahamas with heavy rain and winds of up to 40 miles per hour (64 km/h). The storm then headed for Florida, about 230 miles (370 km) away. As it moved across the ocean, it drew energy from the warm waters below it. Katrina's winds increased to 75 miles per hour (121 km/h). By the time it reached Florida on Friday, August 26, it had become a Category 1 hurricane.

A Quick Strike at Florida

Katrina produced more damage than expected during its swift movement across Florida. As much as 15 inches (38 cm) of rain fell in some areas. Winds toppled trees. Millions of people lost electrical

Naming Hurricanes

The United States began using women's names to identify storms in 1953. Each year the first storm's name begins with an A, followed in alphabetical order by names beginning with the other letters of the alphabet. Beginning in 1979, hurricane names have alternated between male and female names.

If a storm is particularly damaging or deadly, its name is permanently retired. Katrina fits that description. Its name will never be used again.

A car damaged by Katrina in Holland Beach, Florida

power. Fourteen people were killed. Billions of dollars' worth of damage was done.

But Katrina did not linger in Florida. It crossed the tip of the state and headed toward the Gulf of Mexico. It had weakened crossing land and was a tropical storm again. But the warm waters of the Gulf would provide it with more energy.

The Gulf States Prepare

As Katrina left Florida on August 26, it became a Category 3 hurricane. The governors of the Gulf Coast states of Louisiana, Mississippi, and Alabama declared states of emergency. This gave them the power to direct trucks and heavy equipment to areas that would be affected by the storm. They could also order National Guard troops to troubled spots. They could demand residents evacuate and limit travel.

How Hurricanes Form

A hurricane is a huge storm with heavy rains and powerful winds. These storms usually form over warm ocean waters, from which they get their energy. Winds blowing in the same direction and at similar speeds force air up from the ocean surface. As these winds flow outward above the storm, they allow the lower air to rise. This rising motion leads to the formation of clouds. As this humid air rises, it changes from a gas to a liquid. This causes heat to be released into the air, powering the storm further. Winds outside the hurricane steer it. Many tropical cloud systems form each year during hurricane season. But only a tiny number ever have the perfect mix of conditions necessary to become a hurricane.

Louisiana residents board up the windows of a business before the arrival of Hurricane Katrina.

Residents of the Gulf states also prepared for Katrina. They boarded windows and doors with sheets of plywood. They bought extra food, bottled water, and supplies. If they planned to evacuate, they filled their cars with gasoline.

While people prepared for the storm, Katrina stalled over the Gulf's warm waters. It sucked up more energy. By Sunday, August 28, it had become a Category 5 storm with winds of up to 175 miles per hour (282 km/h).

CHAPTER TWO

LANDFALL

On Sunday, August 28, Mayor Ray Nagin of New Orleans, Louisiana, realized his city was about to face one of the most powerful storms in the history of the United States. He instructed all residents to leave the city before the storm struck. Many tried to leave but then found themselves trapped in long lines of traffic. Cars ran out of gas or became overheated. What should have been a two-hour trip

The collapsed water tower of Buras, Louisiana, rests against a destroyed home.

Thousands of displaced New Orleans residents took cover from Hurricane Katrina at the Superdome, a last-resort shelter.

inland to Baton Rouge, Louisiana, turned into a ten-hour ordeal.

The Superdome Becomes a Refuge

Others had no way of leaving the city. Buses were sent to ten locations to bring residents who could not evacuate to the Louisiana Superdome, a large sports arena. By evening, 20,000 people had crowded into the arena to take shelter from the storm. The National

Guard brought some supplies and tried to maintain order. But from the beginning, there was not enough of anything.

A Devastating Landfall

Meanwhile, after gathering strength over the Gulf's warm waters, Katrina headed toward New Orleans. Just before it reached the city, it turned toward southeastern Louisiana. It made landfall on August 29 at Buras, Louisiana. The little town was destroyed by the Category 3 hurricane. Its name on the water tower was almost the only thing

The Louisiana Superdome

Completed in 1975, the Louisiana Superdome is home to the New Orleans Saints football team. The huge steel building has a fixed roof. The structure was designed to withstand winds of 200 miles per hour (322 km/h). Yet Katrina's 145-mile-per-hour (233-km/h) winds blew off part of the roof. After Katrina, the Superdome needed to be repaired. But first, city workers had to remove tons of garbage left behind by the hurricane victims who had taken shelter there.

A flooded truck rests near the destroyed Palace Casino in Biloxi, Mississippi.

left. Fortunately, the entire population, about 3,300 people, had evacuated before the storm arrived.

Katrina Strikes Mississippi and Alabama

Katrina made a second landfall on the Louisiana-Mississippi border. The 450-mile-wide (724-km-wide) storm left behind widespread damage. It battered these coastal areas with its strongest winds and tallest

The Saffir-Simpson Scale		
Category	Wind Speed (mph)	Storm Surge Height (feet)
1	74–95	4–5
2	96–110	6–8
3	111–130	9–12
4	131–155	13–18
5	>155	>18

The Saffir-Simpson Scale shows wind speeds and the height of water surges during each of the five categories of hurricanes. Reread Chapter Two. How high were the storm surges in Mobile, Alabama? Use the scale above to determine what category Hurricane Katrina was at that time. What was the range of its wind speeds at that same time?

swells of water. Its strong winds pushed 30 feet (9 m) of water over the shoreline and flooded almost the entire area. These unusual rises in water during large storms are called storm surges. This flooding ruined buildings of up to two and three stories high. In downtown Biloxi, Mississippi, buildings collapsed due to the storm's force. Katrina ripped apart an almost two-mile-long (3-km-long) bridge across Biloxi Bay.

It scattered the broken pieces of the bridge across a wide area. It chopped up everything in its path. Debris filled the water.

Destruction in Alabama

As it left Mississippi, Katrina pushed surging waters into Alabama. It flooded roads, cars, and buildings in downtown Mobile, Alabama. Floodwaters reached 11 feet (3 m), a foot higher than a regulation basketball hoop. Katrina's winds were not as bad as expected. But they still ripped off roofs, knocked down trees, and destroyed power lines. The state's southwest corner was hardest hit. This piece of land juts into the Gulf of Mexico to form Mobile Bay. In this area, flooding destroyed piers and damaged many homes.

Katrina lost strength as it moved north. But it still had enough power to cause tornadoes and thunderstorms, which often accompany hurricanes.

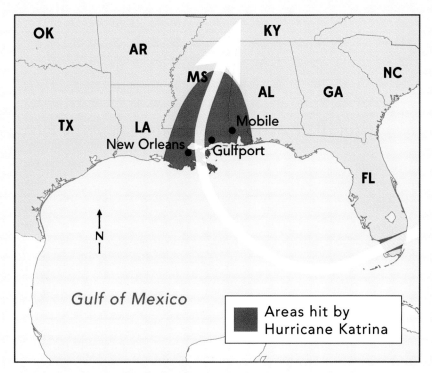

Hurricane Katrina's Path

This is a map of the path taken by Hurricane Katrina. After it stalled over the Gulf of Mexico and became a Category 5 storm, it turned northward. Where would it have made landfall if it had stayed on a straight path after crossing Florida?

False Hope for New Orleans

New Orleans received the back side of the Category 3 storm. Despite destruction caused by heavy winds, the city at first appeared to have escaped major damage. People breathed a sigh of relief. But the worst was yet to come.

CHAPTER THREE

SUFFERING IN NEW ORLEANS

Although heavy winds and rain did strike New Orleans, many at first believed the city had escaped the worst of the storm. Then the lights went out in the Superdome. Generators provided enough power for reduced lighting, but not for air conditioning. The evacuees were miserable in the August heat.

New Orleans residents walk through waist-deep floodwater.

Heavy flooding caused devastation in New Orleans.

Floodwaters caused the Industrial Canal levee to develop a crack. Water began to flow into the east side of the city. At the Superdome, two pieces of metal roofing flew off the building. Rain poured in.

On Monday, August 29, water broke through gaps in two more levees. The city began to fill with water. Gaps in the three broken levees widened. Since most of New Orleans is below sea level, it was very difficult for this water to run off. Most of the city was underwater within 12 hours.

Services Break Down

Officials seemed unsure about what to do next. At the Superdome, the crowd had grown to 25,000. Tempers flared, and fights broke out. There was not enough food or water. The building had become so hot and dirty it was not safe.

On Tuesday evening, the city finally moved some people from the Superdome to the New Orleans Convention Center. However, the move was very unorganized. Conditions at the Convention Center soon became as bad as those at the Superdome. There were still no plans

Levees

A levee is a man-made wall or bank made of dirt, clay, metal, concrete, or other materials. Levees are built to prevent a body of water from flooding an area. Levees range from 10 to 20 feet (3 to 6 m) high. If levees are not cared for properly, they can fail to hold back powerful water surges. Levees that protected New Orleans from both Lake Pontchartrain and the mighty Mississippi River failed during Hurricane Katrina.

to get all the people out of New Orleans. Katrina had choked the city.

As flooding continued, workers had little success repairing the levees. The longer the dirty floodwater remained in the city, the more it filled with smelly garbage and other debris. The pumps used to draw water out of the city were old. Spare parts were not available. Making new ones slowed efforts to pump the filthy water out of the city.

Meanwhile, there were still people who had not been rescued from their homes. Criminals began to steal things and start fires in some areas of the city. Mayor Nagin ordered most of the city's 1,500 police officers to stop search-and-rescue efforts. He needed them to control crime instead. Many residents criticized the police force. In one case, police had plucked people from rooftops and then dropped them on an Interstate 10 overpass. They abandoned the people there with no shelter, no food, no restrooms, and no medical care.

A child looks out of a bus window, waiting to be evacuated from New Orleans.

A Move to the Houston Astrodome

Thousands were still trapped in the Superdome on September 1. Fighting broke out at the Convention Center. Police had trouble controlling the crowds. Mayor Nagin went on national television to beg for help.

Finally, some evacuees began to board 475 buses provided by the Federal Emergency Management Agency (FEMA) to go to Houston, Texas. The trip would take two days. By September 2, the first 15,000 people arrived at the Houston Astrodome. This

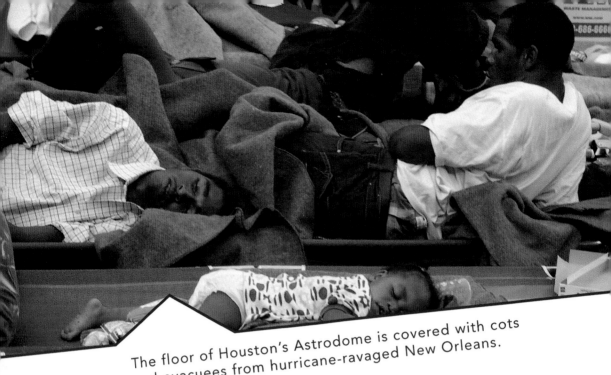

The floor of Houston's Astrodome is covered with cots and evacuees from hurricane-ravaged New Orleans.

facility had air conditioning and clean restrooms. But evacuees feared it would soon become as dirty and hot as the Superdome.

The Astrodome could not handle so many evacuees. Houston mayor Bill White had to open a second facility. And back in New Orleans, thousands still remained in the Superdome and the Convention Center. Bus convoys to Houston continued. On September 3, pilots from a variety of commercial airlines began special flights taking evacuees to Lackland Air Force Base in San Antonio, Texas.

Lupe Flores, a reporter for *Today's Catholic News*, interviewed a woman who had survived Hurricane Katrina. The experiences she shared were chilling:

> *"My six-year-old son, Christopher, kept looking up at the sky and asking, 'Momma, why are the helicopters taking so long? Are we gonna die?'"*

> *With no transportation and no way to get out of New Orleans, the family, who lived in public housing . . . had stayed behind hoping to ride out the hurricane. They huddled together in their upper level apartment when Katrina arrived . . . flooding the lower floor of the building almost up to the ceiling. . . . They stayed in the building for three days. No help came.*

> *"We decided we'd better get out of there . . . the tallest person held my son up on his shoulders so he wouldn't drown."*

> Source: Lupe R. Flores. "Sisters United in Hope after Hurricane Struggle."
> Today's Catholic News *October 5, 2005: 1–2. Print. 1.*

Back It Up

The author of this passage is using evidence to support a point. Write a paragraph describing the point the author is making. Then write down two or three pieces of evidence the author uses to make the point.

CHAPTER FOUR

FACING THE AFTERMATH

Eighty percent of New Orleans was underwater after Hurricane Katrina. The Environmental Protection Agency (EPA) considered Katrina the biggest disaster it had ever faced.

The floodwaters became a poisonous brew of oil, sewage, and industrial waste. The longer the water remained, the more poisons seeped into the ground and groundwater. Officials were worried about lead

The sun sets over flooded coastal wetlands—a haven for water birds—in Venice, Louisiana.

A New Orleans neighborhood destroyed by Hurricane Katrina

and arsenic. They knew that after the water was gone, these poisons would remain in the soil.

Poisonous material settled to the bottom of the water. Engineers removed tons of it as the floodwaters went down. Others worked to tear down buildings filled with mold and debris. That cleanup led to the release of contaminants into the air. People who came in contact with the polluted water and air developed a variety of skin ailments. Many of these problems did not respond to medication. Other workers experienced nausea and vomiting.

The smell of rotting debris, sewage, and chemicals was overwhelming. As the mud dried, poisonous dust swirled through the air. Breathing problems, especially asthma, were common. The vaccines needed to prevent or treat diseases had not arrived. New Orleans was not a safe place.

Meanwhile, announcements about help for Katrina's victims were slow in coming. And when they did arrive, they were often confusing.

Wetlands

The coastal wetlands in the area were also affected by Katrina.

The Environmental Protection Agency (EPA)

The EPA's job is to protect human health and the environment. This agency enforces all federal laws about these subjects. They write the rules that support the laws. They also study and try to solve environmental problems. They provide accurate information about health and the environment in the United States. They help communities with projects affecting the environment. The EPA also monitors the United States' role in working with other nations to protect the global environment.

These two photos show the same area of the Chandeleur Islands, approximately 62 miles (100 km) east of New Orleans, before and after Hurricane Katrina.

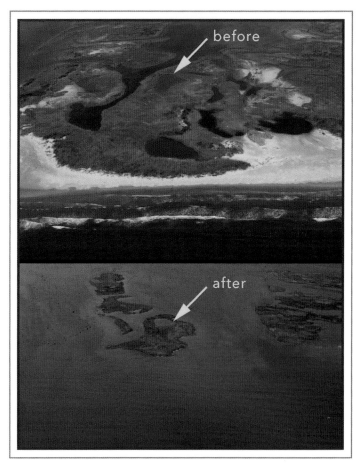

Before the storm, these areas had been home to a wide range of animals and plants. During storms, the wetlands slowed the flow of floodwater, protecting inland communities. The wetlands also cleaned the groundwater by filtering out sediments and pollution.

Before Katrina, erosion had caused the wetlands to lose 10 to 14 square miles (26 to 36 sq km) a year.

Katrina's storm surges made that erosion worse. The salt in the water also killed off a great deal of plant life.

The storm's strong winds blew down huge trees. Birds that had lived in the area moved elsewhere because there were no big trees to nest in. Habitats for animals such as deer also shrank.

The Fishing Industry

Fishing was a major industry along the Gulf Coast before Hurricane Katrina. During the storm, poisons and sewage were released into the water. Storm surges also altered the amount of oxygen in the water. This caused huge numbers of fish to die. The bodies of these dead fish added to the water pollution. Now fishermen could no longer catch healthy fish to sell. Many fishing boats had been destroyed in the storm. Hurricane Katrina nearly destroyed the fishing industry along the Gulf Coast.

A fishing boat washed ashore during Hurricane Katrina lies in Venice, Louisiana.

Facing the Future

Although no one knows for sure what the final tally was, the official number of deaths recorded in New Orleans was 1,836. Another 705 people were listed as missing. Katrina had been one of the nation's deadliest catastrophes.

Katrina left a path of destruction through the Gulf Coast states that devastated both natural and human environments. Recovery efforts would take work and help from government agencies, private groups, and individuals alike.

On August 31, President George W. Bush addressed the nation after viewing the damage caused by Hurricane Katrina from Air Force One:

> *This recovery will take a long time. Our efforts are now focused on three priorities. . . . Our first priority is to save lives. . . . Our second priority is to sustain lives by ensuring adequate food, water, shelter, and medical supplies for survivors. . . .*
>
> *Our third priority is . . . a comprehensive recovery effort. We are focusing on restoring power and lines of communication that have been knocked out during the storm. We'll be repairing major roads and bridges. . . . There's no doubt in my mind we're going to succeed. . . .*
>
> *The country stands with you. We'll do all in our power to help you.*

Source: Douglas Brinkley. The Great Deluge. New York: HarperCollins, 2006. Print. 444–446.

Consider Your Audience

Read President Bush's speech closely. How could you adapt the speech for a different audience, such as your siblings or younger friends? Write a blog post conveying this same information for the new audience. What is the best way to get your point across to this audience?

CHAPTER FIVE

MOVING FORWARD

Hurricane Katrina left behind destroyed property and confusion. Thousands of evacuees were scattered across the country. Many did not know where their family members were, or if they were even alive.

Thousands of people in Louisiana and Mississippi had lost their homes. Property damage was in the billions of dollars. The Gulf Coast states needed

Huge shafts of light shine through the damaged roof of the Louisiana Superdome, littered with debris after serving as a shelter for hurricane evacuees.

FEMA

The mission of the Federal Emergency Management Agency (FEMA) is to take the lead during disasters. During the 1800s, Congress passed a new law that allowed the government to provide help each time there was a disaster. But there was no single, central agency responsible for taking control in emergencies. In 1979 President Jimmy Carter brought all the various disaster relief groups together into one body known as FEMA. While this was an improvement, Katrina revealed the need for FEMA to improve its organization and its ability to respond quickly to emergencies.

to rebuild houses and businesses, repair roads, remove debris, and restore water, gas, and electric service.

In New Orleans, some people had refused to evacuate. Others could not leave because of illness, old age, or lack of money. Most of these people were minorities who lived in the poorest parts of the city. Evacuees wanted to return to their homes to see the damage. But it would be months before many would be able to do so. There was no clean drinking water. Basic

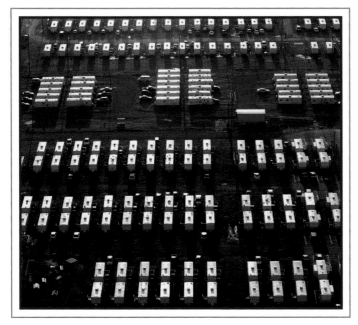

Federal Emergency Management Agency (FEMA) trailers were used to house those left homeless by Katrina.

services such as electricity, gas, and telephones were not working. There were not enough police.

Lessons for the Future

After Katrina, no single organization took charge of the situation in the Gulf states. Agencies at different levels of the government and private charities sometimes seemed to work against one another. The problems responders and victims faced before, during, and after Hurricane Katrina taught both the government and individuals many important lessons about how to prepare for natural disasters.

Visitors enjoy a carriage ride in New Orleans' French Quarter. The city's tourism business is returning to its pre-Katrina levels.

Government officials realized that careful disaster planning is absolutely necessary before a storm strikes. This must include systems for distributing food, water, and other supplies. Evacuation plans must provide for those who do not have their own transportation.

One special law created after Katrina required all disaster plans to include both humans and pets. Other laws provided ways to access loans, medical care, and assistance for children after a disaster. Families and individuals in hurricane-prone areas realized that they needed to have plans too.

Good News

Millions of people came to the coastal states to help after Katrina. Texas cities welcomed New Orleans evacuees. Individuals donated clothing and money. This help lasted for several years.

Today, New Orleans is still in recovery. But the spirit of survival is strong among those who have returned. Gulf Coast residents know that their region will always be at risk for another hurricane. But residents and government officials have made plans to better handle the next big storm to hit the region.

IMPORTANT DATES 2005

Aug. 24

Katrina is named when it becomes a tropical storm.

Aug. 26

Katrina hits Florida as a Category 1 hurricane.

Aug. 26

Katrina becomes a Category 3 hurricane; governors of coastal states declare states of emergency.

Aug. 29

New Orleans begins to flood due to storm surge and rainwater. The flooding worsens as two more levees develop cracks.

Aug. 30

Some of the people sheltering in the Superdome are sent to the New Orleans Convention Center.

Aug. 31

President George W. Bush flies over New Orleans to view the damage. Then he addresses the nation.

Aug. 28

Katrina becomes a Category 5 storm while stalled over the Gulf of Mexico.

Aug. 28

New Orleans, Louisiana, mayor Ray Nagin orders evacuation of the city. The Superdome opens as a shelter.

Aug. 29

Katrina makes landfall south-southeast of New Orleans at Buras, Louisiana, as a Category 3 storm. The first levee cracks in New Orleans.

Sept. 1

Mayor Nagin goes on television to beg for help.

Sept. 2

The first evacuees arrive at the Houston Astrodome in Houston, Texas. Houston mayor Bill White opens the Reliant Center to evacuees as well.

Sept. 3

Evacuees begin to arrive at Lackland Air Force Base in San Antonio, Texas.

Say What?

Studying Hurricane Katrina can mean learning a lot of new vocabulary. Find five words in this book you've never seen or heard before. Use a dictionary to find out what they mean. Then write the meanings in your own words, and use each word in a new sentence.

Another View

There are many sources online and in your library about Hurricane Katrina and its aftermath. Ask a librarian or other adult to help you find a reliable source on Hurricane Katrina. Compare what you learn in this new source and what you have found out in this book. Then write a short essay comparing and contrasting the new source's view of the hurricane with the ideas in this book. How are they different? How are they similar? Why do you think they are different or similar?

Why Do I Care?

Give examples of two or three ways in which the events and ideas in this book connect to your own life. For example, have you or a member of your family ever been in a scary situation like a hurricane or other storm? Have you ever been separated from your family?

Surprise Me

Think about what you learned in this book. What two or three facts about Hurricane Katrina did you find most surprising? Write a short paragraph about each fact. Describe what you found surprising and why.

GLOSSARY

debris
the scattered remains of something broken or discarded

evacuee
a person who evacuates because of danger

hurricane
a rotating storm formed in the tropics with winds of 74 miles per hour (119 km/h) or more, usually accompanied by rain, thunder, and lightning

landfall
the event of a storm moving over land after being over water

meteorologist
a scientist who studies the weather

ordeal
a difficult or painful experience

sea level
the level of the ocean's surface, used to determine land heights and sea depths

storm surge
an abnormal rise in water caused by a storm, with high winds as the major driving force behind the rise

tropical depression
a rotating storm that begins in the tropics and has winds less than 39 miles per hour (63 km/h)

tropical storm
a rotating storm system that forms in the tropics and has winds of 39 to 73 miles per hour (63 to 117 km/h)

LEARN MORE

Books

Hojem, Benjamin. *Hurricanes: Weathering the Storm.* New York: Grosset & Dunlap, 2010.

Tarshis, Lauren. *I Survived Hurricane Katrina.* New York: Scholastic Paperbacks, 2011.

Uhlberg, Myron. *Storm Called Katrina.* Atlanta, GA: Peachtree Publishers, 2011.

Web Links

To learn more about Hurricane Katrina, visit ABDO Publishing Company online at **www.abdopublishing.com**. Web sites about Hurricane Katrina are featured on our Book Links page. These links are routinely monitored and updated to provide the most current information available. Visit **www.mycorelibrary.com** for free additional tools for teachers and students.

INDEX

ABOUT THE AUTHOR

Peggy Caravantes became an author after a career in education. She has published 13 biographies and short nonfiction books. Caravantes is a member of the Society for Children's Book Writers and Illustrators.